T0113613

POEMS
— FROM THE —
UNKNOWN
POET

JEROLD BROWN

Order this book online at www.trafford.com
or email orders@trafford.com

Most Trafford titles are also available at major online book retailers.

Print information available on the last page.

ISBN: 978-1-6987-0686-3 (sc)
ISBN: 978-1-6987-0688-7 (hc)
ISBN: 978-1-6987-0687-0 (e)

Library of Congress Control Number: 2021907603

Trafford rev. 04/13/2021

North America & international
toll-free: 844-688-6899 (USA & Canada)
fax: 812 355 4082

CONTENTS

SO QUIET

So quiet is the morning
That I relax and stare,
So picture-perfect, never boring,
And so beautiful and rare.

So quiet is the day
That it seems lifeless and bare.
So quietly I lay
Without a fear or a care.

So quiet is the night
That I can't wait till morn,
That brilliant light
When a new day is born.

THE MEADOW

The featured green grass that lies beneath my feet
As a cushion on my soles
That presses between my toes so neat
And uplifts all that it controls

Ah, the beautiful meadow
The flowers overflowing
With trees swaying to and fro
And the radiant sun peacefully glowing

To enter would be so nice
The rolling hills
To be in paradise
With the daffodils

To leave would be regrettable
Sad to us that know
That it is unforgettable
The peace that we find in the meadow

THE WIND

The smooth, soft gentle thing that we call the wind
Flows so gently against my face
It moves my hair and refreshes my skin
With its invisible touch
It passes through the open earth
To thrill the wandering creatures
To chill the overheated places
To bring breath to the meadow
To bring ripples to the ocean
To push away those clouds
Blocking my view of heaven
Stretched across the earth so neat
Purifying the fruit so sweet
Going onward
Softly blowing against my face
To move my hair
And to refresh my skin
This invisible touch
That passes through the open earth
Again and again
It's called the wind

THE LAKE

So calmly the water sits upon the lake
With an invisible musk from a misty dew
Captured by every breath I take.
The odorless scent of love in the air, it must be you.

A shadow of darkness falls upon this lusty lake
Filled with feminine pride
With a beauty no man can mistake
And a loved-filled sensation coming from deep inside.

The water is like a mirror as it reflects my face.
The still waters have captured me,
For I am lost in this lonely place,
So I seek a vision to set me free.

I throw a rock across the solid water's bed,
And I wonder where it landed.
There is something snapping in my head,
And it has me stranded.

There across this quiet lake I see you
In a pose that is new to me.
Then you disappear in that misty dew.
And you are forever gone, and this lake will be forever empty.

AT THIS MOMENT

At the moment of truth
As siblings,
We should know
Each other's feelings.

At the moment of unrest
As siblings,
We should feel
Each other's heartbeat.

At the moment as time
Passes by,
We share
The passing of time.

And at the moment,
We stand
As siblings
Interlocked forever.

MY HEART

How greedy is my heart,
For loving so many?
How fragile are my footsteps,
Afraid to step on anyone?
So grateful is my heart
For being loved.
How strong are the footsteps
That lead and carry me?
How desperate is my heart,
For I cannot wait for time?
How my pace quickens,
When I search for an answer.
How strange is my heart,
For the answer is inside?
So I stop and bow,
For my journey is yet to come.

I GRIEVE FOR THEE

The mighty waters that hurt you so.
Oh, New Orleans, I grieve for thee.
How we left you on your own,
Can you ever return home?
Will it ever be the same?
The muddy waters.
The loss of life.
The tragedy.

Oh, America, where did you go,
When your people cried,
When your people needed you,
When your people died?
Oh, New Orleans, I grieve for thee.
All of your pain,
What can I do?
Where are you now?

Can we ever make it up to you?
America, will you try?
Will the street again be lively?
Oh, New Orleans, I grieve for thee.
Mardi Gras, jazz.
Will we play again?
Will we be dancing again?
I grieve for thee.
I grieve for thee.

A DISTANT LOVE

Smiling moon giving brilliant light.
Shining bright on a silent night.
Comfortable beam from high above.
Memories of a distant love.

A romantic mood on a starlit night.
Visible streaks of lovely light.
Visions of a woman, I'll always dream of.
Those wonderful memories of a distant love.

My head hangs under a light-filled sky.
Wondering why my tears went dry.
Surrounded by my lonely shadow.
My mind swaying to and fro

Smiling back at that moon giving brilliant light.
Praying on a silent night.
Floating on a beam from high above.
Memories of a distant love.

The sky opens up; I see her lovely face.
Though time has taken her without a trace,
I'll never hold her again, no, not ever.
I'll never see her again, no, not ever.

I'm led back to earth on a cosmic cloud.
I sit and pray out loud.
I open my eyes to that moon above,
With no more memories of a distant love.

I WANT TO SIT
AND WATCH

I work my field till I sweat,
Then sit on my porch at dawn.
I watch the sun set
And the sky and beyond.

I sit and watch the stars at night,
And the sun comes up in the eastern sky.
The stars are so quiet and polite,
And the sun so brilliant yet shy.

I watch the day pass by
And breathe in the fresh air.
The wind gives her sigh.
The wind and air, what a pair.

I can't wait to watch it unfold again
And dream of our giant sphere.
I want to watch the mountains and meadows blend
And the majestic waters so clear.

I watch nature bring to me,
Our inner universe so great.
All of life's majesty,
And I wait for all the new things
The Lord has yet to create.

SUMMER

Things went along so calm and smooth.
The summer's air so fresh and cool,
Leaving me with a lonely heart to soothe.
Little did I know I'd be played for a fool.

Leaving my feelings aside, I went on,
Trying my best to please,
Yet knowing that these days would soon be gone.
I still felt at ease.

The days passed on, then things got hot.
I'd relax and stare.
Though love was not what I sought,
I still enjoyed the warm summer's air.

Temptation made my feelings come alive,
Though I hid them in the back of my mind.
I fought my innermost drive,
And reality was hard to find.

Then summer had reached her peak.
Feelings had become real strong.
My emotions began to leak,
And I knew summer would not be long.

I wandered around from place to place,
Careless in my actions,
Trapped by summer's feminine lace,
Lost in her attractions.

Fall was coming; he would take her away.
I knew that in spring,
I would be sad on that day.
Was this just a fling?

THE GENTLE AIR

The gentle air
That flows across my face
So freely,
A moment I cannot waste.

The gentle air
That whispers in my ear.
Words of peace,
And so sincere.

The gentle air
That presses against my lips
Begs for advice,
And wisdom tips.

The gentle air
That kisses my brow
With no retreat,
And urging me now.

The gentle air
That up lifts my heart; that is whole.
That gives me strength
And moves my soul.

WHEN I AWAKE

I count the sheep
That run across my eyes
When I lay to down to sleep.
There are still blue skies.

There is a place that we go to,
In dreams.
It takes us from this world, the erotic blue,
As we float on moonbeams.

The faces we try to understand.
The moments we try to keep.
I love all of this, and
Don't wake me while I sleep.

Is it real or just a dream?
There is no confusion of reality to make,
For death will not make me scream,
Because the Lord will be there when I awake.

THE FIREPLACE

As I sit back and watch the glow in my fireplace,
The wood burning hot from the flames of fire,
The glow reflects its shadow upon my face.
Gives me the warmth I truly desire.
In the dark, the silence of the night.
Only my fireplace can be heard.
The wood packed together so tight
Gives a lonely whispered word,
As the sparks jump for joy, as they free themselves
From the wood,
And dance their way into nonexistence.
The fireplaces capture them, just as it should,
And no longer are they seen in the distance.
So there in my fireplace is peace,
When all the flames cease.
So together we shut off our lights.
I my eyes, and he its flame.
We feel the warmth night after night,
And my lovely fireplace is truly the blame.

THE LIGHT
BETWEEN
THE BLACK

When the clouds had come,
And removed the tender blue
With awesome black,
They inlayed was a secrete.

Beyond all that we know,
That we understand,
Is the light between the black.
That makes us wonder.

Yet to know would be to see
Far across the boundaries
Of eternity,
And what lies beyond.

For a moment, that old cloud
Envelops the sky,
Then swiftly passes on,
And then again there is blue.

And no longer fear
For those who don't understand.
And peace for those of us
That do.

THE LIGHT
BETWEEN
THE BLACK II

The black clouds had come again
And turned that blue sky gray.
It looked as if night jumped in
And removed the day.

On purpose we ignore its beauty
Because we think black is bad,
As if it caused a mutiny
On the lovely moment we just had.

Cuddle in despair,
We watch the deepening shade
As if it soaked up our air,
And nothing will come to our aid.

Wondering where it may send me.
Will it bring pleasure or pain?
Watching with envy,
It has the right to maintain.

Now as usual, the lovely wind
Mixes the blue and gray
And blows away the black clouds again.
To settle the changes in our day.

And we no longer ignore
All that beauty,
But ask for more
Without envy.

AUTUMN

A taste of frost upon my lips,
And the fast turning night.
Autumn at last rips
Old summer out of sight.

The falling leaves rest upon the ground,
Covering the changing grass.
Beautiful colors all around.
Intermixing with such class.

Fall has come all so soon.
The days are shortened too,
And the gigantic harvest moon
Settles in the midnight blue.

I love the cool air
And the sky so gray.
Just looking up there
Leaves everything in wonderful array.

I only want more.
I love that autumn day,
Yet I know what I'm waiting for.
Summer is not far away.

THERE IS NO LIGHT
WITHOUT DARK

There is a blanket
That is stretched across the sky,
And the sun's rays peek out
As though to warn us
Of the coming storm,
Or the present light that will
Defeat the storm.
The light brings forth
A new beginning,
As the day goes on.
Time doesn't stop,
And the present seems like
A dream.

Oh, those mighty clouds.
What hides behind them?
And even as they flow
There is still a presence there
Left over like a shadow.
And hard to ignore,
For without it,
What is the meaning
Of the light without dark?

As we press our minds
For an answer,
We stress the thoughts
We have.
What a picture,
Life as it is
There is no light
Without dark.

THE HILLTOP

I looked around
Beyond eternity
Onward
Past the deep blue sea.

In search of what is out there
With the day so bright
Somewhere
In the dark, dark night.

Searching from my hilltop
With my beacon from the past
From the waves that chop
Against the lighthouse so fast.

To reveal the picturesque flow
Under heaven's nest,
And the endless blow
Of breath from north, south, east, and west

Cradled under the noonday sky
Floating on air,
Or resting under those stars so high
I just stare.

Endless is the earth from here,
Day or night,
And so clear
As seen from the hilltop of my house of light.

THE LAST WORDS
OF A DYING MAN

I feel your presence coming closer to me
Though my life is held together by a string.
I think of how beautiful our love could be
And how nothing else would mean a thing.

I feel death coming; my eyes grow dim.
I see a vague vision of a guy you once knew
A guy you once loved, what did you see in him?
I know that's a silly question, but I love you.

I feel my mind begin to float.
I see life no more.
A lump grows in my throat,
And I wonder what I'm crying for.

I love you so badly you do not understand.
A tear runs down my cheek.
How could you love a dying man?
My voice begins to squeak

I see a vision of us together at last.
I see you begin to cry.
That moment went so very fast
Now it is time for me to die.

THE HOUSE

The fresh rain trickled from the roof
The house, the small house I lived in
Was swelling from within
Something inside needed to be released
For a moment, I watched from the window
The bursting thunder from the sky

Some strange force was tugging at my soul
Yet I could not answer my fleeting feelings
The night, the dark, dark night
Held me entranced
The house could not speak
Yet the rain could

An enormous burst and the night lit up
"Come, come to me"
Said the rain
The house held me in
Frightened or needing the security
I stood still

Foreseeing the morning, yet patient within
I see no light
Will day not come?
Or will it come without me?
I fought my feelings
I did not know which was my enemy

The house, the rain, the night
So I went to my bed
Satisfied with my feelings
I would not go
I would not stay
In the house

OH, SAVIOR, HEAR ME

As gentle the air flows
Through my soul so gently
My feelings only the Lord knows
Oh, Savior, hear me.

No soul shall satin raze
May the Lord come swiftly
So that sheep may safely graze
Oh, Savior, hear me.

Tell me, Lord, everything is okay
Take my soul into eternity
And when I pray
Oh, Savior, hear me

Oh, that great day
I will be on bended knee
With my last words I will say
"Oh, Savior, hear me."

THE GHOST
THAT FOLLOWS

I made a path through the knee-high snow
In spring, at the twilight hour
Looking back to see if anyone would follow
For I had an appointment with a supernatural power

I marked the bark of every tree I passed
So I would know which way I had come
Thoughts come and go so fast
Visions of footprints, where do they come from?

I've come so far and keep on going
I go to a place where no one goes
I walk that path not knowing
Yet I feel the presence of the ghost that follows

I'm led by instinct over a hill
To a place so distant yet not too far
To a meadow of hidden daffodils
And the sky had but one star

I breathed in deeply, hoping not to make a sound
And warming up my freezing toes
Clenching my teeth and bearing down
Waiting for the ghost that follows

I peered through the dying night
I made it through my silent woes
Not a creature was in sight
I searched for the ghost that follows

He did not come, so I started down that hill
I saw footprints beside mine in the snow
I ran from that meadow of hidden daffodils
Scared to death for the ghost did follow

For ghosts do prowl during the night
At the break of day they meet their woes
For darkness gives them delight
And that light is how I defeated the ghost that follows.

A-STAR

What am I but a
Budding light
As seen from the earth
At night
Up into the openness of
Heaven above
As a dip of twilight
Filled with love
Eagerly I wish to remain
As day takes me away
But every night I come again and again
A drift in heaven's ocean
So near yet so far
What am I
But a star, a star

MY HEART

How greedy is my heart
For loving so many?
How fragile are my footsteps
Afraid to step on anyone?

So grateful is my heart
For being loved.
How strong are the footsteps
That lead and carry me?

How desperate is my heart,
For I cannot wait for time?
How my pace quickens
When I search for an answer

How strange is my heart,
For the answer is inside?
So I stop and bow,
For my journey is yet to come.

MY EYE TO
HEAVEN

I saw a tear fall from heaven
It brought water to the earth
I saw a star fall from the heaven
It brought light to the earth
I saw a heart fall from the heaven
It brought love to the earth
I heard a voice from heaven
It said,
"Those who feel no love
It will come from above
Those who feel alone
Will feel my presence
Welcome to your new home
Love it, and it will grow
Walk forth and multiply
All things I will give
I will set you free
To be whatever you want
Don't lose focus
Don't hurt your home
Don't hurt each other
For one day you will return home"
I saw a tear fall from heaven
The angels were crying
I saw a star fall from heaven
The earth was on fire
I saw heart fall from heaven
It was broken

Printed in the United States
by Baker & Taylor Publisher Services